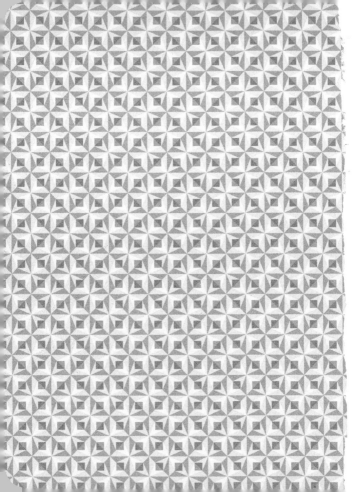

i cannot live without books.

—THOMAS JEFFERSON

recorded by

title:

author:

start date/end date:

my rating (how many stars): ☆ ☆ ☆ ☆ ☆

thoughts:

title:

author:

start date/end date:

my rating (how many stars): ☆ ☆ ☆ ☆ ☆

thoughts:

title:

author:

start date/end date:

my rating (how many stars): ☆ ☆ ☆ ☆ ☆

thoughts:

it is a great thing
to start life with a small number
of really good books which are
your very own.

—SIR ARTHUR CONAN DOYLE

title:

author:

start date/end date:

my rating (how many stars): ☆ ☆ ☆ ☆ ☆

thoughts:

title:

author:

start date/end date:

my rating (how many stars): ☆ ☆ ☆ ☆ ☆

thoughts:

title:

author:

start date/end date:

my rating (how many stars): ☆ ☆ ☆ ☆ ☆

thoughts:

literature is my utopia.

—HELEN KELLER

title: ....

author: ....

start date/end date: ....

my rating (how many stars): ☆ ☆ ☆ ☆ ☆ ....

thoughts: ....

....

....

....

....

title:

author:

start date/end date:

my rating (how many stars): ☆ ☆ ☆ ☆ ☆

thoughts:

list of books i want to read

* from a classic to a recent bestseller or a current-events exposé, make a list of all the books you want to read.

title:

author:

start date/end date:

my rating (how many stars): ☆ ☆ ☆ ☆ ☆

thoughts:

title:

author:

start date/end date:

my rating (how many stars): ☆ ☆ ☆ ☆ ☆

thoughts:

title:

author:

start date/end date:

my rating (how many stars): ☆ ☆ ☆ ☆ ☆

thoughts:

a book is a gift you can open
again and again.

—GARRISON KEILLOR

title:

author:

start date/end date:

my rating (how many stars): ☆ ☆ ☆ ☆ ☆

thoughts:

title:

author:

start date/end date:

my rating (how many stars): ☆ ☆ ☆ ☆ ☆

thoughts:

title:

author:

start date/end date:

my rating (how many stars): ☆ ☆ ☆ ☆ ☆

thoughts:

the proper study of mankind
is books.

—ALDOUS HUXLEY

title:

author:

start date/end date:

my rating (how many stars): ☆ ☆ ☆ ☆ ☆

thoughts:

title:

author:

start date/end date:

my rating (how many stars): ☆ ☆ ☆ ☆ ☆

thoughts:

my favorite authors *

there are some authors you just can't stop
reading. make a list of your favorite writers
and jot down what draws you to them.

title:

author:

start date/end date:

my rating (how many stars): ☆ ☆ ☆ ☆ ☆

thoughts:

title:

author:

start date/end date:

my rating (how many stars): ☆ ☆ ☆ ☆ ☆

thoughts:

title:

author:

start date/end date:

my rating (how many stars): ☆ ☆ ☆ ☆ ☆

thoughts:

real luxury is time and opportunity to read for pleasure.

—JANE BRODY

title: ....

author: ....

start date/end date: ....

my rating (how many stars): ☆ ☆ ☆ ☆ ☆

thoughts: ....

....

....

....

....

title:

author:

start date/end date:

my rating (how many stars): ☆ ☆ ☆ ☆ ☆

thoughts:

title:

author:

start date/end date:

my rating (how many stars): ☆ ☆ ☆ ☆ ☆

thoughts:

a room without books is like a
body without a soul.

—CICERO

title:

author:

start date/end date:

my rating (how many stars): ☆ ☆ ☆ ☆ ☆

thoughts:

title:

author:

start date/end date:

my rating (how many stars): ☆ ☆ ☆ ☆ ☆

thoughts:

my reliable book sources *

do you frequent the library, peruse
bookstores, order online? write down how
you collect most of your books.

title:

author:

start date/end date:

my rating (how many stars): ☆ ☆ ☆ ☆ ☆

thoughts:

title:

author:

start date/end date:

my rating (how many stars): ☆ ☆ ☆ ☆ ☆

thoughts:

title:

author:

start date/end date:

my rating (how many stars): ☆ ☆ ☆ ☆ ☆

thoughts:

today a reader, tomorrow a leader.

—MARGARET FULLER

title:

author:

start date/end date:

my rating (how many stars): ☆ ☆ ☆ ☆ ☆

thoughts:

title:

author:

start date/end date:

my rating (how many stars): ☆ ☆ ☆ ☆ ☆

thoughts:

title:

author:

start date/end date:

my rating (how many stars): ☆ ☆ ☆ ☆ ☆

thoughts:

beware the man of one book.

—SAINT THOMAS AQUINAS

title:

author:

start date/end date:

my rating (how many stars): ☆☆☆☆☆

thoughts:

title:

author:

start date/end date:

my rating (how many stars): ☆☆☆☆☆

thoughts:

quotes to remember *

record your favorite passages, phrases, and
quotes worth remembering and sharing.

title:

author:

start date/end date:

my rating (how many stars): ☆ ☆ ☆ ☆ ☆

thoughts:

title:

author:

start date/end date:

my rating (how many stars): ☆ ☆ ☆ ☆ ☆

thoughts:

title:

author:

start date/end date:

my rating (how many stars): ☆ ☆ ☆ ☆ ☆

thoughts:

to learn to read is to
light a fire; every syllable that is
spelled out is a spark.

—VICTOR HUGO

title:

author:

start date/end date:

my rating (how many stars): ☆ ☆ ☆ ☆ ☆

thoughts:

title:

author:

start date/end date:

my rating (how many stars): ☆ ☆ ☆ ☆ ☆

thoughts:

title:

author:

start date/end date:

my rating (how many stars): ☆ ☆ ☆ ☆ ☆

thoughts:

the answers you get from literature depend on the questions you pose.

—MARGARET ATWOOD

title:

author:

start date/end date:

my rating (how many stars): ☆ ☆ ☆ ☆ ☆

thoughts:

title:

author:

start date/end date:

my rating (how many stars): ☆☆☆☆☆

thoughts:

stories and facts i want to share

* books provide plenty of great insights, clever quips, and fun facts. share the interesting things you've learned in recent books.

title:

author:

start date/end date:

my rating (how many stars): ☆ ☆ ☆ ☆ ☆

thoughts:

title:

author:

start date/end date:

my rating (how many stars): ☆ ☆ ☆ ☆ ☆

thoughts:

title:

author:

start date/end date:

my rating (how many stars): ☆ ☆ ☆ ☆ ☆

thoughts:

the decline of literature indicates
the decline of a nation.

—JOHANN WOLFGANG VON GOETHE

title:

author:

start date/end date:

my rating (how many stars): ☆ ☆ ☆ ☆ ☆

thoughts:

title:

author:

start date/end date:

my rating (how many stars): ☆ ☆ ☆ ☆ ☆

thoughts:

title:

author:

start date/end date:

my rating (how many stars): ☆ ☆ ☆ ☆ ☆

thoughts:

we read to know we are not alone.

—C.S. LEWIS

title:

author:

start date/end date:

my rating (how many stars): ☆ ☆ ☆ ☆ ☆

thoughts:

title:

author:

start date/end date:

my rating (how many stars): ☆ ☆ ☆ ☆ ☆

thoughts:

my favorite places to sit down with a good book *

where do you like to curl up with a book and do your reading—in a cozy café, by the fireplace, on the beach?

_____

. . . .
_____

. . . .
_____

. . . .
_____

. . . .
_____

. . . .
_____

. . . .
_____

title:

author:

start date/end date:

my rating (how many stars): ☆ ☆ ☆ ☆ ☆

thoughts:

title:

author:

start date/end date:

my rating (how many stars): ☆ ☆ ☆ ☆ ☆

thoughts:

title:

author:

start date/end date:

my rating (how many stars): ☆ ☆ ☆ ☆ ☆

thoughts:

reading is thinking with someone
else's head instead of one's own.

—ARTHUR SCHOPENHAUER

title:

author:

start date/end date:

my rating (how many stars): ☆ ☆ ☆ ☆ ☆

thoughts:

title:

author:

start date/end date:

my rating (how many stars): ☆ ☆ ☆ ☆ ☆

thoughts:

title:

author:

start date/end date:

my rating (how many stars): ☆ ☆ ☆ ☆ ☆

thoughts:

until i feared i would lose it,
i never loved to read. one does
not love breathing.

—HARPER LEE

title:

author:

start date/end date:

my rating (how many stars): ☆ ☆ ☆ ☆ ☆

thoughts:

title:

author:

start date/end date:

my rating (how many stars): ☆ ☆ ☆ ☆ ☆

thoughts:

my favorite childhood books

* books you read as a child or young adult can be particularly memorable. write down a few that have stayed with you as you grow up.

title:

author:

start date/end date:

my rating (how many stars): ☆ ☆ ☆ ☆ ☆

thoughts:

title:

author:

start date/end date:

my rating (how many stars): ☆ ☆ ☆ ☆ ☆

thoughts:

title:

author:

start date/end date:

my rating (how many stars): ☆ ☆ ☆ ☆ ☆

thoughts:

a good book is the purest essence
of a human soul.

—THOMAS CARLYLE

title:

author:

start date/end date:

my rating (how many stars): ☆ ☆ ☆ ☆ ☆

thoughts:

title:

author:

start date/end date:

my rating (how many stars): ☆ ☆ ☆ ☆ ☆

thoughts:

title:

author:

start date/end date:

my rating (how many stars): ☆ ☆ ☆ ☆ ☆

thoughts:

great literature is simply
language charged with meaning to
the utmost possible degree.

—EZRA POUND

title:

author:

start date/end date:

my rating (how many stars): ☆ ☆ ☆ ☆ ☆

thoughts:

title:

author:

start date/end date:

my rating (how many stars): ☆ ☆ ☆ ☆ ☆

thoughts:

books i want to write *

for all of those aspiring writers, make note
of your future book ideas, whether they are
memoirs, history books, fantasy fiction,
romance novels, or something else altogether.

title:

author:

start date/end date:

my rating (how many stars): ☆ ☆ ☆ ☆ ☆

thoughts:

title:

author:

start date/end date:

my rating (how many stars): ☆ ☆ ☆ ☆ ☆

thoughts:

title:

author:

start date/end date:

my rating (how many stars): ☆ ☆ ☆ ☆ ☆

thoughts:

reading is to the mind
what exercise is to the body.

—JOSEPH ADDISON

title:

author:

start date/end date:

my rating (how many stars): ☆ ☆ ☆ ☆ ☆

thoughts:

title:

author:

start date/end date:

my rating (how many stars): ☆ ☆ ☆ ☆ ☆

thoughts:

title:

author:

start date/end date:

my rating (how many stars): ☆ ☆ ☆ ☆ ☆

thoughts:

read in order to live.

—HENRY FIELDING

title:

author:

start date/end date:

my rating (how many stars): ☆☆☆☆☆

thoughts:

title:

author:

start date/end date:

my rating (how many stars): ☆ ☆ ☆ ☆ ☆

thoughts:

recommended reading *

suggestions of good books abound. what have
you been advised to read recently, and who
gave you the recommendation?

title:

author:

start date/end date:

my rating (how many stars): ☆ ☆ ☆ ☆ ☆

thoughts:

title:

author:

start date/end date:

my rating (how many stars): ☆ ☆ ☆ ☆ ☆

thoughts:

title:

author:

start date/end date:

my rating (how many stars): ☆ ☆ ☆ ☆ ☆

thoughts:

a book that is shut is but a block.

—THOMAS FULLER

title:

author:

start date/end date:

my rating (how many stars): ☆ ☆ ☆ ☆ ☆

thoughts:

title:

author:

start date/end date:

my rating (how many stars): ☆ ☆ ☆ ☆ ☆

thoughts:

title:

author:

start date/end date:

my rating (how many stars): ☆ ☆ ☆ ☆ ☆

thoughts:

what is wonderful about
great literature is that it transforms
the man who reads it towards
the condition of the man
who wrote.

—E.M. FORSTER

title:

author:

start date/end date:

my rating (how many stars): ☆ ☆ ☆ ☆ ☆

thoughts:

title:

author:

start date/end date:

my rating (how many stars): ☆ ☆ ☆ ☆ ☆

thoughts:

title:

author:

start date/end date:

my rating (how many stars): ☆ ☆ ☆ ☆ ☆

thoughts:

title:

author:

start date/end date:

my rating (how many stars): ☆ ☆ ☆ ☆ ☆

thoughts:

title: ·······························

author: ·····························

start date/end date: ················

my rating (how many stars): ··· ☆ ☆ ☆ ☆ ☆ ····

thoughts: ···························

title:

author:

start date/end date:

my rating (how many stars): ☆ ☆ ☆ ☆ ☆

thoughts:

title: ....

author: ....

start date/end date: ....

my rating (how many stars): ... ☆ ☆ ☆ ☆ ☆ ...

thoughts: ....

....

....

....

title:

author:

start date/end date:

my rating (how many stars): ☆ ☆ ☆ ☆ ☆

thoughts:

of the books i've read *

first book

saddest book

funniest book

scariest book

most inspiring

most influential

favorite literary character

least favorite literary character

literary character i'd most want to date

book setting i'd most want to be my reality

i have always imagined that
paradise will be a kind of library.

—JORGE LUIS BORGES

time to turn a page

cover illustration by nicole kaufman

copyright © 2008. published by clarkson potter/

publishers, random house, inc.

www.clarksonpotter.com

printed in china

isbn: 978-0-307-40723-8

potter style